Herobrine Saves Christmas

Book 3

Zack Zombie Books

Chapter 1
The Weirdest Things

I've realized that over the past few weeks people in the human world have started doing weirder things than ever. It began around the beginning of December with the lights. I know what you're thinking—lights aren't weird—every house has them, right? Well, I'm not talking about the usual lights you see in houses. These were really tiny lights that covered everything.

The first place I saw them was at the mall. At first, I thought the mall just had dandruff. But then I saw them in the trees, in the stores in town and around the outside of people's houses. It looked like the whole town was invaded by radioactive cockroaches.

Apparently, according to Lucy, the lights had something to do with a festival called Christmas. I wish I could say that I understood half of the things that humans in this world do, but this Christmas thing…It really had me confused.

"Hurry up, Herobrine!" Lucy shouted from the bottom of the stairs. "It's the day before Christmas Eve. Mom wants us to run into town to fetch a few things for her. The stores will be packed soon, so let's get going."

I grabbed my scarf and hat and trudged down the stairs. December was a cold time of year in the town where Lucy Lurker and her family lived, and I didn't really care for it. I much preferred hotter climates. In fact, I'd happily take up residence beside a lava river in the Nether.

As I reached the bottom stairs, Mrs. Lurker came running up to me really excited about something.

"Oh, Herobrine! How exciting is this? It's Christmas Eve tomorrow. This is your first Christmas ever! How do you feel?"

"Cold!" I replied, trying to muster a smile upon my frozen face. "Why is it so cold in here? What's happened to the heating?"

"Broken!" Mr. Lurker murmured from the large chair in the living room. "Broken until this afternoon. Then, it'll be fixed."

Mr. Lurker was a man of few words. Normally all that ever came from him were grunts and groans.

"Right, now you have my list, dear," Mrs. Lurker said, zipping up Lucy's coat. "If you don't get everything on it then don't worry, but try to do your best."

"Will do, Mom!" Lucy replied, opening the door and stepping onto the porch. She tilted her head at me and gave me a glare that said, "Let's go!"

I could tell Mrs. Lurker was proving to be a bit annoying for Lucy as usual, so I hopped down the last stair and out of the house.

"Finally!" Lucy gasped. "Free!"

Lucy bounded into the street and headed towards town with me in tow, as I tried desperately to wrap my scarf around my head a few more times. Anything I could do to keep the cold out was a bonus.

"So, what's your Mom got on her list?" I asked Lucy.

"Let me see...A ham...a turkey..."

"A turkey? You getting a new pet?" I asked.

"No, silly. A turkey for Christmas."

I nodded like I knew what she meant. But honestly... I had no idea what she was talking about.

"... a new star for the tree and one of those annoying singing Santa statues."

Lucy looked at me and smiled as we approached Main Street. Now, ham I could understand... I knew what that was. The pet turkey thing confused me and I had no idea why she needed a new star for a tree. But, I had another question that was really messing with my freezing brain.

"Hey Lucy...What's a Santa?"

"Santa? Are you serious?" Lucy laughed. "You don't know who Santa is?"

"Is he made out of sand?" I asked, trying to take a guess.

"You really don't know anything about Christmas do you?" Lucy said giggling. "Santa is a really happy fat guy with a white bead who wears a red suit. He lives in the North Pole and brings presents to all the boys and girls around the world every Christmas."

"Wow!" I exclaimed excited to hear the story about a fat guy with a beard that brings toys.

"But, if he's so fat, how does he get around so fast?" I asked.

"He has a wooden sleigh and some reindeer."

"Reindeer. What's that?" I questioned.

"Reindeer are like big horses that can fly. They pull the sleigh through the air."

I stopped in my tracks as Lucy continued down the street. The world I came from was filled with Withers, Creepers and Zombie Pigmen, yet this Santa guy and his flying horses seemed weirder than all of them put together.

I looked up for Lucy, but she must have gone into one of the shops, because I couldn't see her anywhere. I glanced around town. Not only were there fairy lights everywhere, but little silver strings hung inside the shops and banners hung in the windows saying 'Merry Christmas'.

As I looked up at the town clock, all of a sudden I heard singing. I hadn't heard anyone singing in the town before. It was probably because the noise they were making didn't sound so good. But, I followed the noise anyway, to see where it was coming from.

I walked to the end of the first block and turned the corner to be greeted by three grey-haired men and three grey-haired women all trying to sing together. The women wore silver strings in their hair and each of the men wore a red hat with a fluffy white ball on the end.

A few people were standing around watching, so I decided to join them.

When the song finished some people clapped and some people moaned, but they all threw things into a bucket that sat on the floor in front of them. I thought I should too, so I put my hand into my coat pocket, pulled out a half-eaten sweet potato and threw it in. I turned to leave when suddenly someone grabbed my scarf and yanked me back.

"What's the meaning of this?" one of the grey-haired men said, shoving the sweet potato in my face. "We're collecting for charity here!"

I had no idea who Charity was, but looking at how mad everybody got, I guessed she must not like sweet potato. Luckily, Lucy appeared by my side to save me.

"It's okay, Mr. Squawker," she said. "This is Herobrine. He's not from around here. He didn't mean any harm."

The man let go of my scarf and Lucy threw some money into the bucket. I figured holding people's scarves for ransom was how these old folks made money for their friend Charity.

The moment he let go I backed away, trying to loosen the scarf and regain circulation in my head.

"What was all that about?" I asked Lucy.

"Those are Christmas Carolers," Lucy explained. "They were singing Christmas songs to raise money."

"I thought people were giving money to Charity, not Carol," I said.

Lucy just looked at me funny, gripped my hand and headed down the street.

"What's in that bag you're carrying?" I asked, spotting a bag she didn't have earlier.

"It's the ham," Lucy replied. "One thing checked off the list, three to go."

We stopped by the curb on the opposite side of the street next to a huge toy store.

"What do we need from the toy shop?" I asked.

"Nothing!" Lucy replied. "It's just the best toy store in town, so I thought we could have a look. Come on!"

Lucy pulled me across the street towards the huge double doors of Mr. Windup's Wondrous Toy shop. There were massive red bows on the windows on either side of the door and the really big displays full of toys.

As the double doors automatically opened I could feel the excitement rise inside me — partly because I wanted to check out all the toys but mainly because I saw some big square toys that looked just like me.

As we went in, I had a feeling that the toy shop was going to be my kinda place...

Chapter 2
Mr. Windup's Wonderous Toy Shop

"**W**elcome, one and all to my marvelous, magical toy shop, filled with wonderful, hand-made toys for young and old, meek and bold!"

I looked to my left as we entered and a short man in a top hat and weird colorful clothes greeted us.

"My name," he continued, "is Mr. H. P. Windup and this is my shop."

The man was one of the weirdest characters I had ever seen. He wore a pink waistcoat, a bright blue shirt underneath and pants with a red line running down the side. He looked like

a circus clown who had just slipped and fell into a bucket of jelly.

He was standing on a small podium and jumped down as the doors swung shut behind us.

"I know you! You are Lucy, correct?" he said, raising his hat and bowing to greet her, "but who is this intriguing looking square fellow?"

"This is Herobrine," Lucy replied. "He's a good friend of mine."

"Ah! Any friend of Lucy Lurker is a friend of mine," Mr. H.P. Windup said, shaking my hand. "You're a blocky chap aren't you?"

I didn't quite know how to reply to that comment...

Mr. Windup stepped behind us and moved into the middle, putting his chubby hands on our shoulders. Then, he slowly moved forwards and started taking us on a personal tour.

"This toy shop has been in the Windup family for three generations," he said proudly. "We do not import toys here. Everything you see before you is hand-made by Windup workers."

I stepped closer to a shelf and picked up what was called a 'JACK IN THE BOX.' I couldn't find the 'JACK' part, but I did find a cool windup handle, so I decided to turn it...

Then... I found Jack.

As I was getting up off the floor, beside me was a rocking horse that was hand-made too. I had never seen a rocking horse before. Closest thing back home was a horse skeleton that I saw floating in a lake once. I tried to ride it, but it was really hard...especially over the waterfall.

"Through the back we have some of our work-shops," Mr. Windup said, leading us towards a large door with 'NO ENTRY' written across it in red.

As we went through it was hard to see anything but people. The place was packed!

As I squinted into the sea of workers I could spot workbenches, and on those workbenches were rows of toys being carved and put together.

"It's like Santa's workshop in here!" Lucy said.

"What do you think, Herobrine?" the eccentric toy shop owner said, turning to me. "Bet you've never seen anything like this before?"

I shook my head. The place was terrifying. I had never seen so many humans in one place before. It smelled funny too.

"You look like a handy sort of fellow?" Mr. Windup continued. "I bet you're good at building things."

"Yep. I am!" I said proudly.

"I thought so. Well, tomorrow is Christmas Eve and all the workers in here will not be in the factory. Today is their last day. However, I need someone in the workshop just in case we get any last minute toy requests. Fancy working here with me tomorrow?"

I looked a Lucy. She shrugged her shoulders. It seemed she could see no reason why I couldn't help out for a bit.

"Perfect! Make sure you're here at the bright and early. The chances are I won't need you, but you never know."

With that, Mr. Windup led Lucy and myself back into the main shop and then headed off to speak to another customer.

"Looks like you're coming back here tomorrow then," Lucy said, patting me on the back. "It's probably a good idea. Mom gets even weirder on Christmas Eve. You'll probably be safer out of the house."

We left the toy shop and headed back out onto the street. Lucy looked at her list. She took out a pencil and crossed off the 'Singing Santa' statue. She looked at me and frowned. There was obviously no way she was going to try to find one of those after all.

"We'll just tell Mom we couldn't find one." she whispered as she winked at me. I didn't know what to do so I just winked back. But it was pretty hard since I didn't have eyelids.

17

We walked down the sidewalk to a store that seemed to sell nothing but Christmas decorations. There was a large, gleaming star in the window.

"Wait here," Lucy said as she disappeared through the solid white door of the Christmas store.

I took a step to the side and looked in through the window. Lucy was chatting to the shop assistant. The assistant walked over to the window, leaned through and plucked the gleaming star from the display. She headed back to the desk, took some money from Lucy and then handed over the star, which Lucy promptly put into the bag with the ham.

I stepped back to the door as Lucy walked out.

"Just need to get the turkey," she said, pulling out the list from her pocket for the final time.

I looked up and down the street.

"There doesn't seem to be a pet shop in this town," I said.

"We don't need a pet shop," Lucy responded. "We need a butcher."

I had no idea what a butcher was, but I assumed it was a shop that sold pet turkeys.

As we entered the butcher's I froze in my tracks. After looking around the butcher shop, I realized that humans do some weird things to their pets.

Then I saw a wall poster that really creeped me out. It said that humans should eat three square meals a day. After seeing what they do to their pets, I didn't want to find out what they would do to a square guy like me. So I decided to wait for Lucy outside.

Meanwhile, Lucy approached the butcher, who she seemed to know. They shared a joke and then the butcher handed over a large bag filled with something extremely heavy.

The butcher looked out the window in my direction with a confused look on his face. But, I was used to that by now.

As Lucy came out of the butcher's, she thrust the large heavy bag into my arms.

"Here, you can carry this," she said.

I gripped the bag tightly but I couldn't hold on to it. I had no idea that a pet turkey would have been so heavy. So I just put it on my head, then everything was fine.

With all the items checked off of the list, we walked back through town in the lightly falling snow towards Lucy's house.

"Are you prepared for the next crazy Christmas event in the Lurker household?" Lucy asked as we walked along. "It's Dad's favorite part of Christmas."

"What's that?" I asked, having no idea what was coming next.

"Once we drop these at home we're all going to jump in the car and head off to buy a tree."

"A tree?" I asked. "But you have loads of trees. You have four in your front yard and about ten behind your house."

"Ah, but this tree will be going in our living room."

I frowned at Lucy, thinking she must be joking. After all, how ridiculous can you get?

A tree in the living room, that's silly, I thought.

This Christmas thing was getting weirder by the minute.

Chapter 3
The Christmas Tree

As we approached Lucy's house, Mr. Lurker was outside throwing some long, thick ropes into the trunk of the car.

"Going spelunking, Mr. Lurker?" I joked using the latest word I learned on TV.

Mr. Lurker didn't say anything. He just snarled and grunted at my comment. I realized he was born with a real shortage in the sense of humour department.

I followed Lucy up the steps and into the house. As we entered Mrs. Lurker came rushing over.

"So, where is it?" she cried, unable to contain her excitement.

"Herobrine has it," Lucy replied.

As the only thing I was holding was the pet turkey, I assumed Mrs. Lurker was talking about that.

I moved into the kitchen and slid the turkey off my head onto the kitchen counter.

Mrs. Lurker immediately placed it on a scale and sighed with happiness. "Perfect!" she said. "This will be the biggest turkey we've ever had for Christmas dinner."

Dinner? Man, humans and their pets are so weird, I thought.

Just then, a loud shouting noise came from outside followed by the honking of a car horn.

"Is anyone coming to get this tree with me or not?!!"

It was Mr. Lurker. He was obviously in the car and ready to go.

Mrs. Lurker jumped for joy and ran to fetch her coat.

I began to take my scarf off until Lucy grabbed my arm.

"What are you doing?" she asked with a look of confusion on her face.

"Well, I was thinking I might stay here. After all, there are plenty of trees in the garden for me to look at. I don't see how coming with you guys to get another one will be too exciting."

"Ah! That's where you're wrong!" Lucy replied, grabbing the end of my scarf and wrapping it back around my neck. "A Christmas tree is a special thing and picking out the right one is even more special. Come on!"

Mrs. Lurker opened the front door and I followed Lucy through to the porch. Her Mom closed the door and the three of us joined Mr. Lurker in the family car.

Mr. Lurker grunted as the last car door slammed shut. Then, he threw the car into reverse, almost running over a stray cat that was walking by.

Mr. Lurker then crunched the gearstick and we moved away down the street in the opposite way to the town. Soon, all civilization seemed to be behind us. I wondered where this special tree was going to come from.

After we drove for around ten minutes, Mrs. Lurker came up with a suggestion.

"Why don't we all sing some Christmas carols?" she said with delight.

"Why are we singing songs about Carol again?" I whispered to Lucy. "And where's Charity? Is she coming?"

Lucy just looked at me with the normal confused look she gives me.

Suddenly, without further discussion, Mrs. Lurker burst into song.

"Deck the halls with 'boughs' of holly..."

Lucy quickly joined in, as so did Mr. Lurker.

It was the first time I'd heard Mr. Lurker come close to anything that sounded joyous. But, even with his best try he still just sounded constipated.

Since I had no idea why they were singing about 'bowels,' or what a 'Falalalalalalalala' was, I just looked out the window as we drove along.

The snow had stopped and up ahead I noticed some lights rising into the quickly darkening sky. It seemed we were almost there.

Within a few minutes, Mr. Lurker made the announcement.

"Well, here we are!" he exclaimed. "Terrance Toptrees' Tree Lot."

He pulled the car into the almost empty parking lot and switched off the engine.

As the engine stopped it sputtered and coughed. It didn't sound healthy at all and I was concerned that it would never start up again.

"It always does that." Lucy whispered, noticing the worry on my face. "Dad's had this car for as long as I can remember. He's too cheap to buy a new one."

"Good evening, Lurkers!" said a jolly man who came strolling out from a small hut to greet us. "How are you all on this Christmas Eve, *eve?*"

"We're good, Terrance," replied Mr. Lurker, shaking the man's hand. "We're here to find our tree."

"Well, you've come to the right place," Terrance chuckled. "All I have here are trees... and a fresh hot cocoa in my hut!"

Either the wind was blowing too hard or I just heard him say he had fresh hot cocoa in his butt.

Terrance led the way through some gates to a huge area filled with nothing but pointy trees. I took a look around. They all seemed exactly the same to me.

"We really want a big tree this year," Mr. Lurker said to Terrance as he walked over to see some trees.

"I think a medium one will do," Mrs. Lurker whispered into Terrance's ear when Mr. Lurker looked the other way.

Terrance showed us some of his best trees. Then, Mr. Lurker picked one out and Terrance pulled it from the line and dragged it towards the car. With Mr. Lurker's help, Terrance lifted the tree onto the roof of the car and took some money from Mrs. Lurker.

"Can we get in the car, Dad?" Lucy asked, rubbing her arms. "It's freezing."

Lucy was right. As the sun disappeared the temperature had dropped suddenly with it.

We climbed into the car, and I only hoped the heating system at their house would be fixed by the time we got home. Someone was supposed to be coming while we were out, so hopefully we'd be returning to a warm house.

I climbed into the back of the car with Lucy as Mr. Lurker took the ropes from the trunk, threw them over the tree and tied it in place on the roof. Then, he jumped in and turned on the car. It sputtered, spat and even coughed. But it finally started, and we headed home... singing more Christmas songs on the way.

As we got home we could see the boiler repair van backing out of the drive. Lucy gave me a high five. It appeared that the heater was fixed.

The moment the car pulled up, we jumped out and ran into the house. The place was warming up nicely, which was great because Lucy and I were almost frozen.

"Herobrine, can you go outside and help Lucy's father get the tree in? I'll get the hot cocoa," said Mrs. Lurker, taking off her coat and boiling the kettle. "Lucy, you can bring the decorations in from the study."

I wasn't too happy about going outside again because it was so cold outside and I was warm and toasty inside. But I knew it was the right thing to do.

When I went outside I could hear Mr. Lurker moaning and groaning, and saying words that I really didn't know the meaning of. It seemed that getting the tree down from the top of the car was not as easy as it looked.

"Hey Blockhead! Come here and help me get this tree in the house," Mr. Lurker said, frustrated.

"You push on that side and I'll pull on this end," Mr. Lurker said as he walked to the other side of the car. As Mr. Lurker walked over, I noticed that because my hands and arms were really cold, it gave them more sharp edges.

I used one edge of my arm to see if I could cut
the ropes off the tree. It worked. The tree fell
right over. Unfortunately, the tree fell right
on top of Mr. Lurker. From all of the strange
words he was using, I don't think he was very
happy.

After Mr. Lurker dragged himself from under
the tree, we picked it up and headed for the
door.

"You push and I'll pull," Mr. Lurker said as he stood in front of the doorway. But no matter how much we tried, we couldn't fit it through the door.

"Let's switch places," Mr. Lurker said. So I stepped in front of the doorway and he got on the other side. This time it was harder than before. I kept pushing like he told me, but I didn't understand how Mr. Lurker expected to get the tree in that way.

Humans are so weird, I thought.

After twenty minutes, we decided to switch places again. This time, it worked. I figured it was a better idea this way, but I didn't want to offend Mr. Lurker by saying so.

We dragged the tree into the living room and pulled it in front of the window before dropping it on the floor.

"Careful not to drop the pine needles everywhere, dear," Mrs. Lurker said, spotting a

trail of small, green tree needles on the floor between the hall and the living room.

"I can't stop them dropping off the tree, you know," Mr. Lurker replied with more frustration.

"Hey, Blockhead!" Mr. Lurker said as he began to lift the pointed end of the tree into the air. "Help me lift this tree into the holder."

In front of the window was a wide tube with four legs jutting out from it. We lifted the tree into the air and thumped it inside. Then, he stood back and looked.

I stared at the Lurkers. Mr. Lurker put his arm around his wife and daughter and they all smiled.

To be honest, the whole thing was really weird. I didn't see the point in staring at a tree in the living room when there were plenty of trees in the garden. Plus, the ones in the garden were bigger too, so the entire situation made no sense at all.

"I guess it's time to put the ornaments on," Mrs. Lurker said.

Then, once they had taken in the sight of the tree, they each opened up some old boxes and pulled the treasures out.

There were treasures of all kinds. Silver and gold shiny balls and jewels of all different shapes and sizes, and they were all really glittery.

Lucy handed some lengths of silver string to me.

"What's this?" I asked, thinking I'd struck it rich.

"That's tinsel. You hang it on the tree," she said. "It's good fun."

I took the tinsel and started placing it on the tree. All I could think about was how much I could trade it in for back home in Minecraft.

Once the tinsel was on, they hung the shiny balls and placed all the little jewels on the tree too. Finally, it appeared to be finished.

"Just the star now!" Mr. Lurker said, pulling the newly bought star from the packaging.

He handed it to Lucy and lifted her up. She placed the star on the top of the tree and then the entire family stood back as Mrs. Lurker dimmed the lights.

The fairy lights on the tree glowed, sending sparkles flashing off of the tinsel and shiny balls.

Mrs. Lurker had tears in her eyes. I thought it was probably because of all the money they were throwing away by putting all their treasures on a dumb tree.

Humans are so weird, I thought.

I helped Lucy put the empty treasure boxes away as Mr. and Mrs. Lurker brought out dinner. Then, it was off to bed. I knew I needed to get a good night's sleep. I was going to be helping out at Mr. Windup's toy shop early the next day and I had a feeling it would be harder work than it sounded.

Chapter 4
Christmas Eve

I woke up to the sound of Mrs. Lurker clattering away in the kitchen. I looked over at Lucy's bed. She was fast asleep. She was obviously more used to the early morning commotion than I was.

I stretched, threw on my clothes and headed downstairs.

"Good morning, Herobrine," Mrs. Lurker said as she cleaned the best plates and prepared them in a pile for Christmas dinner the following day. "Happy Christmas Eve!"

"Thanks, Mrs. Lurker," I replied, before heading to the refrigerator to get some cake. As I pulled out a slice, I looked out the window and noticed a thin layer of snow that lay on the ground which made the yard look like the winter biomes back home. However, there was something in the yard that caught my eye. It was a strange looking statue that I hadn't seen before.

I took a bite of cake and strolled over to the back door. I opened it up and looked at the statue. It looked like some sort of gnome or elf, with a pigs face. I hadn't noticed it before and it looked out of place. I hadn't seen Mr. Lurker get it down from the attic, but I assumed it must be something they had put out there at some point yesterday.

"Will you shut that door, Herobrine! You're letting all the warm air out," Mrs. Lurker said, rubbing her arms.

I closed the door, finished my cake and thought no more of it. I went to the front door and put on my scarf and shoes.

"You're heading out early," Mrs. Lurker said, craning her neck around the kitchen doorway to see what I was up to.

"I'm helping Mr. Windup in the toy shop today," I replied. "I'm going to be in charge of making the toy orders that come in at the last minute."

"It probably won't be too busy," Mrs. Lurker shouted as she vanished back into the kitchen.

"Most people put their orders into Mr. Windup weeks ago. Everyone will just be collecting their finished toys today."

I opened the front door hoping Mrs. Lurker was right. The idea of hanging out in a toy shop on Christmas Eve seemed like a good idea...as long as there wasn't any work to do.

I closed the door behind me and looked up at Lucy's room as I headed down the street. Her curtains were still closed. She was obviously enjoying a good sleep in. It was Christmas Eve after all, so I guess that was allowed, especially as I'd heard that everyone gets up super early on Christmas Day.

As I approached Main Street the town was beginning to get busy. Cars were driving up and down, and people were shouting "Merry Christmas!" to one another across the street. The signs that hung in the store windows were being spun from 'CLOSED' to 'OPEN' and there was a really strange but magical feeling in the air. I hadn't felt anything quite like it before.

Soon, I made it to the toy shop. People were beginning to mill around on the sidewalk outside, but the store was still closed, so I made my way through the growing crowd and knocked on the double doors.

A scrawny looking teenager opened the door slightly and stated they were closed.

"I'm Herobrine," I replied, pushing my square foot inside the door before he could close it. "I'm here to help Mr. Windup. I'm working in the store today."

The scrawny kid looked me up and down, opened the door halfway and then pulled me in and slammed the door closed behind me.

"We have to be careful at this time on Christmas Eve," the boy said. "People will be piling through those doors in a few minutes, and it'll be a race to get the best toys that are left. We have to be careful not to let anyone in before 9am!"

The boy glanced at the clock on the wall and then turned and vanished down a long aisle of toys before turning and moving out of sight.

All of a sudden, Mr. Windup appeared by my side as if from nowhere.

"Good morning and a happy Christmas Eve to you, young Herobrine!" Mr. Windup bellowed, causing me to jump. "Are you ready for a fun day?"

"I guess so," I replied.

"I should hope so! Everyday is fun here at my toy shop."

I smiled as I took off my scarf. After all, the toy shop was much warmer than it was outside.

Just then, Mr. Windup glanced at the clock on the wall.

"One minute until opening time!" he said. "When those doors open it will be a stampede in here. Let's get you to safety."

Mr. Windup led me quickly to a desk that had a sign hanging above it saying 'TOY ORDERS HERE!'

"Now, just stand behind this desk and take any orders from people who want to have toys made," Mr. Windup said, patting me on the shoulder. "I'm not really expecting anyone to place any orders today because it's Christmas Eve. But, if they do, you'll be the one to make them as the workshop staff has the day off."

With that, the clock struck nine and Mr. Windup dashed to the double doors to welcome the customers. I stared at the doors as they opened. Mr. Windup was right. A stampede had begun.

The doors were flung open and a crowd of people came streaming into the shop. Luckily, none of them seemed to be heading my way.

There were parents and grandparents rushing to every toy aisle I could see. They were pushing and shoving to get the last remaining

toys from the shelves. A long line began to
form at a desk on the other side of the store
where people waited to collect toys they had
ordered days and weeks ago. Then, one partic-
ular woman caught my eye. She was a heavy
set woman with horn-rimmed spectacles and
really red lipstick. She was looking around and
then seemed to be making her way towards me.

I assumed she needed help and was ready
to point her in the direction of the informa-
tion desk. However, before I could get the
first words out of my mouth, the rather scary
looking woman leaned over the desk towards
me and spoke.

"I need robot soldiers!" she stated.

"Err... robots are in aisle twelve," I muttered,
looking at a map of the shop floor on a sheet
of paper on the desk.

"I don't think I'll find what I'm after out there,"
the woman continued. "That's why I've come to
you."

It was becoming difficult to hear the woman as the noise in the store intensified.

"Have you even looked?" I asked.

"How rude!" the woman replied. "What I require I certainly will not find on the shelves of this toy shop," she insisted. "I shall need to order them."

"But it's Christmas Eve!" I replied. "That means we'll have to make your order today."

"Exactly!" said the woman. "You'd better get on with it. I can't be hanging around in here all morning."

I grabbed a pencil and looked for some paper. There was none on the desk, so I turned over the map of the shop floor and scribbled on the back.

"I require toy robot soldiers," she stated again as I wrote her order down. "They must be 1 foot high."

I was in such a panic to write down her order that I pressed too hard on the pencil and the tip broke. I tried to continue to write. I took the small tip that broke off and tried to write with that, but my square fingers made it really hard.

"And I need six hundred of them."

I scribbled away... robot soldier, 600, 1 foot tall...

Just then, a man walked past carrying a toddler. The toddler was holding some juice and the kid squeezed the carton, and the juice shot out all over the paper. I rubbed my arm across it to clean it off. I could still just about make out the scribbles, but the paper was now wet and soggy.

"Have you got all that down?" the woman asked, adjusting her spectacles. "I'll be back to collect them later on. They are for the poor children of the town, so don't mess this up!"

I frantically tried to scribble her order down again but the paper was wet and ripped as I pushed the pencil over it.

"What's you name?" I asked, looking up, but the woman was gone. I caught sight of her rather large behind disappearing out through the double doors that only just accommodated her.

I was in a panic. I left the desk and ran around the shop trying to find Mr. Windup, but it was no use. The shop was so busy I could hardly make my way through the swelling crowd.

I decided I had to manage this order on my own. I ran back to my desk, put a sign on the top that said 'CLOSED' and made my way towards the workshop door at the back of the store. There was a small glass window in the top of the door. I could see that inside it was pitch black.

I pushed the door open and it clattered shut behind me. I flicked the light switch on the wall and the rows of lights flickered on, illuminating a hundred workbenches, each equipped with basic tools and a lamp. I pulled up a stool to the nearest bench, climbed up and put the piece of paper on the workbench. I clicked on the lamp and positioned it over the paper. I re-read the order as best I could, but the pencil had faded with the juice and my writing was really hard to read.

"100 robot soldiers. Each one 6 feet high," I said out loud.

100 soldiers? That's not so bad. It was only 10 am, so I knew with my building skills, I could get it done in no time.

I decided the first thing I was going to need would be the materials. I jumped down from the workbench and spotted the material rooms. I could feel my heart beating faster in my chest. The pressure was on. There was no way I was going to disappoint 100 poor kids. I knew there and then, I had to get the job done. Robot soldiers, here we come!

Chapter 5
Robot Soldiers Complete ! !

I threw open the door of the material store-room as quickly as I could. The moment the door opened the lights came on inside and I dashed into the room.

In front of me were rows and rows of metal shelves, each containing sheets of plastic, wood and metal. Against the wall were trays of nails and screws. There was even a bench with some strange equipment.

The materials were pretty heavy, so I dragged them through the workshop and leaned them up against my workbench. Then, the real work began.

I thought I'd start off by making one and then, if that went well, I could use that as a model for the other ninety-nine.

The lady didn't say what she wanted them to look like, so I had a hard time deciding how to start. I looked in the full length mirror on the wall and started talking to myself about what to do. All of a sudden, I got the really good idea of what they should look like. Then I started working.

I looked at the clock and finished my first
robot soldier by almost 11am. The robot looked
awesome. It towered into the air, almost hitting
the ceiling.

"Okay!" I whispered to myself. "Now the
production line begins!"

I cut out loads of body parts, heads, legs and
arms and lay them out on every spare workbench surface I could find. Then, I ran around
with the glue, fixing all the parts together.
Then, I connected the eyes and the battery
packs to power them. Finally, I had to glue on
the hands and feet.

By the time I was finished, I had so much glue
on me that my fingers were practically stuck
together. I stood back to observe my work. It
looked like at a Minecraft Army!

I ran to the sink, washed the glue from my
hands and checked the time — it was just after
4pm. I ran out of the workshop, back into the
toy shop and headed towards my desk. The

shop was due to close at any moment and I was sure that the large, scary woman would be hovering there, waiting to collect her order. Sure enough, the woman was there and as impatient as ever!

"Ah! There's the square young man!" the woman thundered to Mr. Windup who was standing beside her. "This is the boy who took my order. Are they ready for collection?"

I was out of breath, but nodded.

"Wonderful!" the woman boomed, looking around. "Where are they? Are they boxed up and ready to go?"

"Uh...they're too big for boxes," I said.

"What do you mean too big? Haven't you got boxes large enough to take them?"

"I don't think they make boxes that big," I said.

The lady and Mr. Windup both gave me a really strange look. *Did they have boxes that big?*

I thought. Well, there was only one way to find out.

"I'll bring one out so you can take a look."

I went to the back workshop and prepared one of the soldiers. I pushed the button on the robot's back and its eyes glowed red.

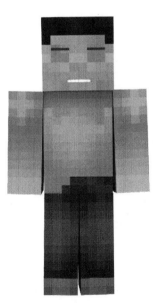

She's going to be so excited when she sees these!

It started marching through the workshop doors in front of me. As we got through the workshop doors, the lady gasped.

"What is this?!!" she yelled, "I said 600 soldiers, one foot tall!"

I pulled out the crumpled piece of paper from my back pocket and read out the order. "100 robot soldiers. Each six feet tall."

"What? Stupid boy! Why would I want one hundred, six foot tall soldiers? They're bigger than me! No, no! I ordered 600 robot soldiers that are one foot tall. Come on! Where are they?"

I turned and glanced back at the workshop.

"Out of the way!" the woman boomed. "I'll come and collect them myself."

The woman pushed past me and headed towards the workshop with Mr. Windup flapping after her.

I stood where I was and just watched as the woman pushed the door open and then almost fainted.

"My goodness! What a disaster!" she screamed. "This is terrible, absolutely terrible! The poor children of the town can't have these. They're useless!"

The woman thundered from the shop with Mr. Windup groveling behind her every step of the way. She pushed through the double door, becoming momentarily lodged, and then cannoned out into the street and out of sight.

Mr. Windup locked the doors behind her. All of the staff on the shop floor were just standing and staring at me.

"What have you done?" Mr. Windup asked.

"I did what she ordered. I'm sure I did."

"Why would she order robots that were so large? Kids can't play with those," Mr. Windup said, disappointed.

After Mr. Windup mentioned it, the idea of six foot tall toy robot soldiers did seem a bit strange.

Mr. Windup took off his top hat, wiped his big forehead and sighed.

"Well, let's get these useless robot soldiers to the dump at the back of the store. They can get picked up on Monday," he said, signaling to his staff to help him carry them. I stepped forwards to help.

"Ah! I think you've helped enough for today," Mr. Windup said, looking slightly upset. "Head home, Herobrine."

I collected my scarf and made my way to the doors. I felt really bad.

I opened the door and prepared to close it behind me, but before I did, Mr. Windup called out to me.

"Hey, Herobrine. Merry Christmas."

He smiled, trying to cheer me up after obviously seeing how upset I was. Then, he disappeared into the workshop with the rest of his staff and began lifting out the robot soldiers.

I hung my head and trudged off down the street towards the Lurker's house. I couldn't believe it. It was my first Christmas and it seemed that I'd ruined it for everyone.

Chapter 6
Kidnapped !

I stood outside the Lurker's house as the sun set. I could see Lucy and her parents laughing and joking inside. I knew the moment I stepped into the house they'd ask me how my day was. I didn't want to spoil the mood. They seemed so happy. I took a deep breath, walked up the steps to the porch and opened the front door.

"Hey! It's Herobrine!" cried Lucy. "Come on in and join the fun!"

Lucy was dancing with her mom and dad to some Christmas songs in front of the Christmas tree.

"I'm okay, thanks. I think I'll just head upstairs for a bit."

"Don't be silly!" said Mrs. Lurker, grabbing my arm and pulling me in for a hug. "It's Christmas Eve. It's time to relax and enjoy yourself."

I took off my scarf and threw it onto the couch.

"So, how did it go at the toy shop today?" Lucy asked with a big smile on her face.

"Okay." I replied, trying my best to lie. "It was busy. I just want some time alone."

I wandered through to the kitchen and out through the back door to the yard. I hung my head and sat on the bench. A few minutes later the door opened again and Lucy stepped out.

"What's wrong?" she asked as she sat beside me and put her arm on my rectangular shoulders. "Bad day?"

I nodded. "I messed up a huge order for 600 poor kids. Now, they won't get any Christmas presents and it's all because of me."

"Come on," Lucy said. "It can't be that bad!"

"I took an order that should have been for six hundred, one foot tall robot soldiers, but I made one hundred, six foot tall robot soldiers!"

"Oh boy. Yeah, that is pretty bad."

I hung my head further. Lucy obviously didn't know what to say next, so we both sat in silence.

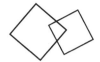

I could feel my feet getting colder by the minute as they rested in the thin layer of snow on the paving.

Suddenly, Lucy sat upright beside me.

"You okay, Lucy?" I asked, seeing a strange, concerned look upon her face.

"No," she replied. "What is that?"

I turned to see where Lucy was pointing. She was pointing at the weird pig-faced gnome statue in the yard. Except this time it was closer to the bench.

"I think it was some sort of weird Christmas tradition. Maybe your dad put it out here last night."

Lucy got up from bench to take a closer look. She crouched down and stared into its eyes.

"I've never seen it before in my life," Lucy said, looking over the object. "It looks a bit like you, Herobrine... all square and weird."

"Gee, thanks," I said.

Lucy sighed and then sat back on the bench beside me. "Guess Dad must have brought it. Creepy statue though. Don't think Mom would approve."

Lucy went to put her hand on my shoulder again, but before she could the bench suddenly tipped backwards. I climbed to my feet and shook my head. It was then that I noticed that the gnome statue was gone!

I looked around for it quickly, assuming we had knocked it over as we fell, but it wasn't there. Then, something appeared behind me. It grabbed my arm, pulling me sideways, and it did the same to Lucy before she even had the chance to fully steady herself.

Next thing we know we're being stuffed into a large sack.

"What's going on?!!" Lucy cried.

"No idea." I replied. "But I think that gnome has come to life and it's attacking us!"

As the gnome creature dragged us through the garden towards the back gate I knew I needed to get a better look at our kidnapper.

I was able to cut a hole in the sack with my cold finger, and when I looked through it, to my amazement, I was staring straight into the face of a Zombie Pigman.

Before I had the chance to ask what it was doing here, it dragged us both through the back gate and into the dark passageway beyond. It moved behind the houses, pulling me and Lucy in the sack with him.

"It's a Zombie Pigman!" I cried out.

"A Zombie what?"

"Pigman! It's from my world. It must have been disguising itself as a gnome. That's why it looked to weird."

"What does it want with us and how did it get here?"

"I have no idea!"

The Zombie Pigman began to move faster. It looked over its shoulder to be sure we weren't being followed. It appeared the Minecraft mob had a plan.

Suddenly, it stopped in front of a gate. It kicked the gate with its leg and pulled us up the stairs of a house. Then it kicked open a large door.

I was about to cry out for help when I couldn't believe my eyes. As I looked through the hole in the sack, I could see that there, in the middle of the library of this house was a gigantic Minecraft Portal.

"We're at the house again!" I whispered. "The one I came to on Halloween. The one with the portal... We're in Herobrine's Mansion!"

"Wait... You have a mansion?" Lucy asked.

"No, it's not my mansion. It's Herobrine's Mansion."

"But you are Herobrine," Lucy said.

"Not me. The other Herobrine," I said.

"There's another Herobrine?" she asked.

But before I could answer, the Zombie Pigman dropped the sack on the floor. Then it grabbed it tightly again and moved with calm determination towards the glowing portal.

"The Zombie Pigman must have found a way of getting into your world," I said.

"So what do we do now?" Lucy panicked.

At that moment I had two thoughts going around in my head. First, I was actually quite looking forward to going home again. And second, I was worried for Lucy. If we went through that portal she might never get home.

But before I could ponder my thoughts any longer, the Zombie Pigman jumped into the portal, taking me and Lucy with him.

"AAAAAHHHH!!!!" was all we could say as we went through the portal.

Everything was fuzzy, then it all went black. We had left the human world behind and what lay waiting for us on the other side filled me with complete dread and excitement at the same time.

Chapter 7
Into the Nether

My vision began to come back as we leapt out of the portal and into the Nether. The moment we hit the ground the Zombie Pigman let go of us and we tumbled out of the sack and onto the floor.

I looked across at Lucy. She had transformed into a box-shaped figure like me. I decided not to draw her attention to it. Being kidnapped by a Zombie Pigman and transported into the Nether was serious enough without alerting her to the fact that her body shape had completely altered.

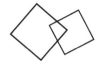

"What do you want?" Lucy yelled, taking a step back from the Zombie Pigman. "Why have you kidnapped us and brought us here?"

The Zombie Pigman looked worried. I could instantly see now that he meant us no harm.

"My name is Piggers Swinely," it said quietly. "But you can call me Piglet. Everybody else does. I didn't mean to frighten you, but I had no choice but to do what I did."

"What? You mean hiding in my parent's garden pretending to be a creepy gnome, knocking us off a bench, putting us in a sack, dragging us into a weird house and pulling us into another world?" Lucy screamed.

"Uh…Yes, that!"

"Try to keep your voice down," I said. "There could be some seriously hostile mobs around here. We don't want to let them know we're here."

Lucy grunted. She now seemed as annoyed at me as she was at Piglet.

"I need your help," Piglet continued. "We have a serious problem. Santa Claus has been captured by a Wither."

The moment he said those words, Lucy's mouth dropped open. I knew she had no idea what a Wither was, but if Santa had been captured and brought to the Nether on Christmas Eve then she knew things were serious.

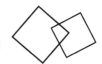

"The Wither took him from your world while he was going over his list of naughty and nice kids. It dragged him through a portal and is holding him in a prison in the Nether Fortress."

Lucy was in a panic. "If we don't get Santa back to my world then he won't be able to deliver everyone's presents tonight! Christmas will be ruined!"

Lucy and I agreed there and then that we had to track down the Wither as quickly as we could. I knew the Nether well, because I used to live here with my parents. So I took the lead with Lucy and Piglet following behind.

The Nether was a treacherous place, with dark caverns and bubbling lava rivers. I took Lucy's hand to keep her safe as the temperature in this dark world began to rise.

Then, in the distance I saw the Nether Fortress. I couldn't see anyone near it, but as we looked up, flying above the Nether Fortress was a really big Wither. It looked really mad and appeared to have someone or something captured inside a prison.

"Santa must be in there," I said.

"What is that thing?" Lucy asked.

"That's a Wither," I said. "It's deadly, menacing and has really bad breath."

"It has three heads!" Lucy cried.

"All Withers do," I said.

"Where are its legs?"

"It doesn't have any. It kinda just bobs around," I added.

We began to move towards it slowly, hiding behind any rocks we could find. We finally entered the Nether Fortress and made our way to the prison. The Wither was hovering next to the prison really excited about its prize prisoner.

"How can we get a good look inside?" Lucy asked.

"We'll have to distract the Wither," I said.

"Squeak! I'm afraid!" Piglet squealed.

"Lucy, you wait here with Piglet. I'll go over there and try to lure the three-headed mob away."

I left Lucy and Piglet behind the prison and dashed off down another corridor in the Fortress. Then, I began making noises that echoed throughout the Fortress.

The Wither looked toward my direction. The noises got its attention and it decided to come and check them out.

As the Wither moved towards me, I peered carefully around the edge of the corridor. The Wither had moved away from the front of the prison and Lucy made her move. She crept quietly to the front of the prison and gazed in through the barred window in the door.

However, the moment she did, the man inside let out a colossal noise. "Ho, ho, ho! Who are you, little girl?!!"

It seemed this Santa fella was one of the loudest people I have ever met.

Suddenly, the Wither turned around and bounded back towards the prison. As soon as Piglet saw it coming, he darted down one of the corridors, but Lucy was slower to react and tripped and fell in front of the prison. The Wither loomed over her.

I had no time to lose. Lucy was in serious danger. I ran to the prison and jumped to her side.

"Stop!" I cried, throwing myself between Lucy and the Wither. "She is from the human world. She means no harm. The fat, jolly man in the red suit you've captured means a lot to the people of her world. We want to get him out of this prison and return him home!"

"Never!" snapped the middle head of the Wither. "Do you know what this Santa guy has done to me? All my life he has forgotten about me, bringing me nothing but terrible presents while my brothers got the best presents every single year."

"You?!! I got the worst presents ever!" cried the Wither head on the left.

"You two don't know the meaning of the word unfair," the other Wither head on the right said. "Last year Santa brought me a sled, and I was forced to share it with you guys!"

Next thing we know the Wither heads were arguing amongst themselves.

"The reason you guys don't get good presents is probably because you're all so mean and nasty!" Lucy cried, climbing to her feet.

The Wither hissed with anger. "I'm as good as any other Wither!" the middle head growled.

"Not better than me!" the left Wither head yelled.

"Oh yeah? Well, I'm better than the both of you," the right Wither head exclaimed.

Then the Wither's started arguing again.

"Maybe if you guys weren't so selfish," Lucy replied, "maybe Santa would have brought you what you asked for."

Lucy moved over to see if she could run, but by now the Wither was really mad.

It quickly swooped in front of Lucy, knocking her back. It loomed over her again, hissing and shaking. Then, the Wither shot through the roof of the Nether Fortress making a giant hole in the roof as it flew out.

It let out a loud high-pitched scream.

"EEEEEYYYYAAAAAEEEEEEE!!!!!!"

Its cry echoed across the whole of the Nether. It shook the lava in the river and more Nether bricks fell from the Fortress roof.

Gradually the echo faded away, but in its place came something far more terrifying. As I looked through the Fortress window, I could see on the horizon a mass of black mobs marching toward us.

I squinted to get a better look as they moved into focus. They were moving rapidly towards us. It appeared the Wither had called for reinforcements. Dozens of angry Wither Skeletons were on their way.

It seemed their mission was total destruction. And that included destroying me, Lucy, Santa and destroying Christmas once and for all!

Chapter 8
To the Rescue !

The Wither Skeleton army was advancing faster than I had expected. I looked to Piglet for help, but he was running away at top speed into the distance. It appeared he didn't want to stick around for the fight. So it was going to be up to me and Lucy to save Santa, and save Christmas for all of the people in her world. However, if we were going to defeat a Wither Skeleton army, I knew we'd need an army of our own.

"Stay here!" I cried to Lucy as she stood there with her mouth open.

"Stay here? Where are you going?"

"I have to go back!"

"Back where?"

"Back though the portal. We need an army to defeat these Withers."

"Do you know someone in the army or something?" Lucy asked.

"No. Something even better!"

With that, I took one last look at Lucy, gave her a smile of reassurance and then sprinted back across the Nether towards the portal as quickly as I could. As I ran I heard Lucy calling out my name in the distance. I felt terrible for leaving her, but I knew we had no other choice. If Santa and Christmas were going to be saved, this would be the only way to do it.

Soon, I couldn't hear Lucy's voice any longer. Part of me feared for her safety, yet I was hoping she and Santa could evade the Wither and his Wither Skeleton army long enough until I got back.

I looked straight in front of me. There it was. The portal was glowing with a purple haze. As I got to it, I closed my eyes and jumped through it.

I felt like I went into a spin as the portal sucked me through and spat me out in to the human world. I tumbled onto the floor in the library of the mysterious house. I knew where I needed to go. I just hoped I could get back to the Nether in time.

I sprinted through the front door, through the gate and stood in the dark passageway. I ran onto the street and then I ran all the way into town.

I made it all the way to the Mr. Windup's toy shop. I ran around to the back of the store where the dumpster was. And there, right in front of me was exactly what I wanted.

Piled up in front of my eyes were one hundred, six foot tall robot soldiers.

I grabbed the first one, stood it up and pushed the button on its back. Its eyes glowed red.

They still work!

I did the same with the next one, and the next. I kept going until the last of the 100 robot soldiers was standing in battle ready position. I was completely worn out, but I needed to head over to the portal as soon as possible to save Lucy, Santa and Christmas before it was too late.

When we made it to Herobrine's Mansion and made a bee line straight for the portal. As soon as we were in front of it, I gave a final salute to my new army and we marched into the portal.

I dizzily re-emerged in the Nether, got to my feet and looked around. And behind me marched the one hundred robot soldiers. Their eyes glowed red and they were ready to follow me into battle.

I let out a war cry and sprinted towards the Nether Fortress in the distance. I led the army past the long lava river and past caverns until we made it to the Nether Fortress prison. Unfortunately, by the time we arrived, the Wither army was ready for us too!

My robot soldiers rammed into the Wither Skeletons at a colossal rate and the battle to save Christmas began!

It seemed my robot soldiers were a good match for the menacing Wither Skeletons. They hurled their thick arms at the mobs as the mobs hissed and pounced in retaliation. The red robot soldier's eyes glowed brighter and then fired laser beams at our attackers. As each Wither was struck it exploded in a ball of light and disappeared.

I wanted to get to the prison to free Santa. If we could get him out while the battle was in full swing, we could take him to the portal and the Wither wouldn't even notice.

"Herobrine!" Lucy cried as she crept out of her hiding place. "You came back! I kinda thought you were going to leave me here."

"No way. I just needed to go back for a little help," I said.

Lucy gave me a big smile. But then I remembered I had to save the jolly fat prisoner in the red suit.

"Let's get Santa!" I shouted to Lucy over the noise of the fight.

We crawled along the ground, trying to evade the gaze of the Wither Skeletons, or of the Wither who was bouncing up and down in the air, shooting Wither skulls at my soldiers.

When we reached the prison door, we peered inside. Santa was by the door.

"Ho, ho, ho! And who are you my square friend?"

"No time to explain Santa. Just be ready to run as soon as I open the door," I said.

I kinda felt bad for Santa. As chubby as he was, I knew he ran he wouldn't get very far.

I took a deep breath and placed my hand on the door, but it was locked. I pulled as hard as I could, but it was no use.

"Herobrine, your eyes!" Lucy said.

What? Did she think I was crying or something?

"No, your eyes!" she said using two fingers pointing to her head.

My eyes? I touched my eyes to see what she was talking about. My eyes were burning hot. I think all the excitement must've activated them.

"Stand back Santa!" I said.

I focused my eyes as best as I could on the prison lock, and BLAM! White beams shot out of my eye sockets and blasted the door right off of its hinges.

As I went to get Santa, all of a sudden the Wither shot a Wither skull beside me that blasted me a few feet away, and knocked me to the ground.

A horrifying shadow loomed over me. I looked at the Wither as it hovered over me and I wondered if this was the end... Was this the end for me, the end for Lucy, the end for Santa, and the end of Christmas?

Chapter 9
Freeing Santa

I could see nothing but the massive Wither that towered over me preparing a Wither skull to hurl at me. As it unleashed its Wither skull blast, I thought it was all over. Suddenly, one of my robot soldiers jumped in front of me, and the Wither skull blasted the robot soldier into a million pieces.

I turned to look at Lucy, but to my surprise, she wasn't there. In all the confusion I had totally lost sight of her.

Then, as the Wither seemed like it was about to end my existence with another Wither skull blast, I heard a noise coming from one of the Nether Fortress corridors. The Wither looked up. There, in front of the corridor entrance leading outside was Lucy. She was making noise to attract the Wither and it seemed to be working. It pounced toward Lucy. The Wither's anger appeared to be intensifying as it sped towards Lucy as quickly as it could.

I whistled to two robot soldiers who were standing nearby. Lucy needed rescuing and fast.

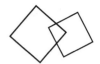

They ran after the Wither as quickly as they could and managed to catch up just as it reached the corridor entrance that led out of the fortress.

Lucy ran for cover as a battle ensued in the entrance of the Nether Fortress between the Wither and the two robot soldiers. The Wither sent blast after blast that missed the soldiers but hit the Nether Fortress, shaking to its foundation. Then one of the blasts hit a robot soldier, blasting him through a wall and shaking the entire fortress, sending Nether bricks tumbling down.

Then, it blew the other robot soldier against the other side of the Nether Fortress. This time there was an even larger crash. The Nether Fortress was beginning to crumble as the Wither stood in the entrance and prepared to fly after Lucy.

While the robot soldiers were distracting the Wither, Santa and I made it out of the Nether Fortress. But after the Wither defeated the robot soldiers it went after Lucy. Lucy had no choice but to run back into the crumbling Nether Fortress.

As she ran in, the Wither flew quickly after her.

What is she thinking? Doesn't she know this place is about to collapse!

But as she was running through the corridor, I could see her waving at me through the Fortress windows. She was pointing at her eyes again.

Are her eyes starting to hurt or something? I thought.

Then I figured out what she was trying to say. As crazy as it was, I realized that it just might work.

The Wither was getting closer and closer to Lucy as she ran to the other side of the corridor that also led outside.

As she was on her way out, I was concentrating my eyes on the biggest pillar that was barely holding up the entire Nether Fortress. My eyes started getting red hot and then smoke started coming out of my eye sockets.

As soon as Lucy made it outside she yelled.

"NOW!"

I released what I think was the most powerful eyebeams that have ever come out of my head.

"BLAAAAAAM!"

My eyebeams hit the pillar with so much force that it disintegrated. All of a sudden, the entire Nether Fortress came crashing down.

Before the Wither could escape, the fortress crashed down all around it, trapping it inside. And as the dust cleared I could still hear the Wither hissing with anger. It was trapped and had no way to escape.

With their master defeated, the few remaining Wither Skeletons ran to the Nether horizon as quickly as they had arrived.

Lucy ran to my side and she gave me a great big hug.

"We did it!" she said as she hugged me and Santa.

I was so happy I got up and started dancing.

"Oh yeah! We did it! We did it! We did it!" I said doing my Herobrine shuffle.

Then Lucy and Santa eventually joined in.

"Oh yeah! We did it! We did it! We did it!" they yelled as they joined in.

After our little celebration, the Nether became quiet. The only sound was the bubbling of the running lava that flowed through the molten rivers.

"Ho, ho, ho! Merry Christmas!" Santa chuckled as his belly bounced up and down like a bowl full of jelly.

"Thank you Lucy and Herobrine for rescuing me. You've been a very good girl and very good...err...boy this year."

"No problem, Santa," I replied.

"Ho, ho, ho! Now, could one of you tell me the time, please? I have a busy night ahead of me and I don't want to be late."

"I don't know," Lucy said. "But it's after dark."

"After dark?" Santa panicked. "My goodness. I must get going. Can you show me the way back to the human world so I can find my sleigh? It's Christmas Eve, you know, and I have things to do!"

Lucy and I laughed and led Santa back to the portal.

"What is this contraption?" Santa asked.

"It's a portal," I replied. "The Wither brought you to the Nether through it. It's the only way back."

I took Santa by the hand and he gripped ahold of Lucy's hand too. Then, on the count of three, we all jumped into the glowing purple portal.

We landed with a thump back in the library of the mysterious house. We had made it. We had traveled to the Nether and rescued Santa.

Santa looked up at the clock on the mantelpiece.

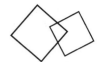

"Goodness me! It's almost midnight!" he said. "I must get going."

We followed Santa into a small wooded area at the back of the house. All of a sudden Santa gave a whistle, and before we knew it a star swooped out of the sky and landed in front of us. It turned into a sleigh pulled by eight funny looking flying horses.

"Wow! Is this your sleigh and reindeer?" Lucy asked, running her hands over it.

"It certainly is, Lucy," Santa chuckled. "Now you two, get yourselves off to bed. If you're not in bed by midnight then I can't deliver your presents, now can I?"

We gave Santa a hug, but as we did he must have caught sight of my unhappy face.

"What's the matter, Herobrine? You've done a wonderful deed and its Christmas tomorrow. You should be happy!"

"I'm afraid I've ruined Christmas for six hundred poor children in the world," I replied. "You see, I was supposed to make..."

"Yes, yes!" Santa interrupted. "I know all about it. Don't worry my square young boy. Leave it to me."

And, with that, Santa climbed aboard the sleigh, signaled to his reindeer and they shot off into the night sky, leaving a trail of magical dust glittering behind them.

Lucy and I stood in the wooded are for a few minutes until the glitter faded. Then we walked back down the streets, into Lucy's garden, into her house and up into bed. As we climbed under the covers Lucy checked her clock. It was ten minutes to midnight. I closed my eyes tightly. It had been a busy day and I couldn't wait for Christmas Day to arrive!

Chapter 10
Santa Saves the Day

"Wake up! Wake up!" cried Lucy, shaking me vigorously. "It's Christmas morning. Get out of bed. Let's go and see what Santa brought us."

We ran downstairs as quickly as we could in our pajamas, with my square feet pounding on each step, making it sound like a thunderstorm.

The moment we entered the living room we were greeted by Mr. and Mrs. Lurker who were both in their thick, red robes.

"You two have slept in a bit this morning," said Mrs. Lurker, giving us both a huge hug. "That's not like you, Lucy. Usually on Christmas you're the first one up."

"You must have had a busy day yesterday, eh Blockhead?" Mr. Lurker chipped in.

"Yeah! You could say that," I laughed.

After the Christmas Day hugs were completed, Mr. and Mrs. Lurker moved aside and revealed an incredible sight. There, under the tree was a small mountain of presents. Lucy and I rushed towards them, knelt down and began to read the tags. They all seemed to be for us.

I began ripping the wrapping paper form the boxes and over the next half an hour we opened up every present we had. I couldn't believe how lucky I was to be spending Christmas with an amazing family like the Lurkers. However, a part of me still felt sad. I had ruined Christmas for so many poor children. I had to admit, I was surprised that Santa had brought me any presents at all.

As I was pondering this thought, the doorbell rang.

Mrs. Lurker answered the door. I could hear a woman outside speaking. Suddenly, the hair on my square neck stood up as I recognized her voice. It was the woman with horn-rimmed spectacles whose order I had messed up at the toy shop.

"Err... Herobrine?" called Mrs. Lurker, leaning back into the house. "Can you come here for a moment, please?"

I slowly rose to my feet and began to make my way towards the door. What had I done now? Surely I hadn't created another disaster? Maybe the woman had brought all six hundred children to the Lurker house so I could see how sad they were. After all, why should I enjoy my Christmas when I'd ruined it for so many others?

I walked toward the door, took a deep breath and then faced the enemy.

The heavily set woman blocked out almost all the sunlight as her large frame filled the porch.

"Ah, ha! Herobrine, young man," she said. "I want to show you something."

It seemed she had brought some of the children to our doorstep. I gritted my teeth and prepared for the onslaught of crying faces. I wondered what I would say.

However, as the woman stepped to the side, the sea of faces that greeted me were happy. Not only that, but each of the children were holding a one foot tall robot soldier that looked like me, with glowing red eyes.

"It seems you have somehow saved the day," Mr. Windup said, stepping into view. "Did you manage to get back into the workshop and make all of these last night? It seems like an impossible task!"

"Ah! That would explain why he was so tired this morning," Mr. Lurker said.

"Is it true, Herobrine?" Mrs. Lurker asked. "Are all these children holding these toys because of you?"

I didn't know what to say. Yes, I had had something to do with it. After all, if Lucy and I hadn't saved Santa then Christmas would never have arrived for any of us. However, I didn't want to take the credit for delivering all those robot soldiers.

"Santa must have brought them," I said.

The children cheered and the woman and Mr. Windup laughed.

"Well, wherever they've come from, the children and I want to truly thank you," the woman said. Then, she leaned forwards and kissed me on the cheek.

Now, even though a kiss on the cheek from that creepy lady wasn't really the Christmas present I had been after, seeing those happy children meant more to me than anything.

Then, suddenly in the distance we heard a faint noise.

"Ho, ho, ho! Merry Christmas!"

We looked up to the sky and many miles away we could see a moving object. Suddenly, it shot across the sky at a rapid speed and vanished out of sight, leaving an arc of glittering dust behind it.

This had been my first Christmas in the human world, and it would be one that I would never forget.

The End

And

Merry Christmas!

Leave Us a Review

Please support us by leaving a review.
The more reviews we get the more books we
will write!

And if you really liked this book, please tell
a friend. I'm sure they will be happy you
told them about it.

Check Out Our Other Books from Zack Zombie Publishing

The Diary of a Minecraft Zombie Book Series

Get The Entire Series on Amazon Today!

The Ultimate Minecraft Comic Book Series

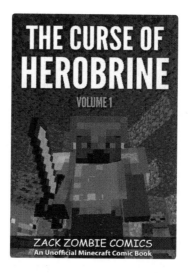

Get The Entire Series on Amazon Today!

Herobrine's Wacky Adventures

Get The Entire Series on
Amazon Today!

The Mobbit

An Unexpected Minecraft Journey

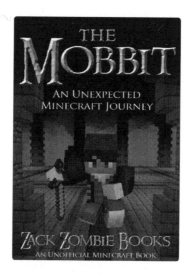

Get The Entire Series on Amazon Today!

Steve Potter and the Endermen's Stone

Get The Entire Series on Amazon Today!

An Interview With a
Minecraft Mob

Get The Entire Series on
Amazon Today!

Minecraft
Galaxy Wars

Get The Entire Series on
Amazon Today!

Ultimate Minecraft Secrets:
An Unofficial Guide to Minecraft Tips, Tricks and Hints to Help You Master Minecraft

Get Your Copy on
Amazon Today!

Made in the USA
Middletown, DE
24 May 2016